W9-ASZ-490

Making Music

6
Instruments
You Can Create

by Eddie Herschel Oates

illustrated by Michael Koelsch

HarperCollins*Publishers*

Making Music
6 Instruments You Can Create
Text copyright © 1995 by Eddie Oates
Illustrations copyright © 1995 by Michael Koelsch
All rights reserved. No part of this book may be used or reproduced in any
manner whatsoever without written permission except in the case of brief
quotations embodied in critical articles and reviews. Printed in Mexico.
For information address HarperCollins Children's Books, a division of
HarperCollins Publishers, 10 East 53rd Street, New York, NY 10022.

Library of Congress Cataloging-in-Publication Data
Oates, Eddie Herschel.
    Making music : 6 instruments you can create / by Eddie Herschel
Oates ; illustrated by Michael Koelsch.
        p.   cm.
    Summary: Includes instructions for making a variety of simple musical
instruments from ordinary household items.
    ISBN 0-06-021478-3. — ISBN 0-06-021479-1 (lib. bdg.)
    1. Musical instruments—Construction—Juvenile literature.   [1. Musical
instruments—Construction]   I. Koelsch, Michael, ill.   II. Title.
ML460.018   1995   92-20060
784.192'3—dc20   CIP
                                                                     AC MN

Typography by Christine Hoffman
2   3   4   5   6   7   8   9   10
❖

To Christine
–EHO

For Matt and Liane
because of their help and inspiration.
–MK

Introduction

Music is found everywhere, from the sounds made by a symphony orchestra to the wind whistling through the trees. Add to the wind in the leaves the sound of one limb striking another, and then a bird call, and nature has produced music.

Making your own music is a lot of fun! In this book, you will learn how to make all kinds of instruments, using materials you probably have around your house.

Instruments you bang on to make sounds are called *percussion* instruments. A drum is a percussion instrument that has a hollow body with one or more openings covered by a surface, known as a skin, that vibrates when it is struck. The vibration of the skin makes the drum's sound.

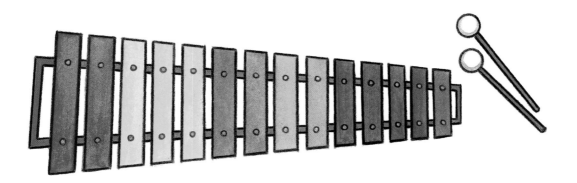

Another percussion instrument is the xylophone. The xylophone's sound is made when its bars of wood or metal are hit with a special hammer. Using this book, you can make a *balloon tom-tom drum*, a *wrench xylophone*, and a *xylo-drum*.

Instruments that you blow into, or that use the air around them to produce sound, are called *wind* instruments. A trumpet is a wind instrument and so is a trombone. When air is blown into the trumpet's metal tube, it creates a sound that gets louder when the air passes through the funnel-shaped end of the instrument.

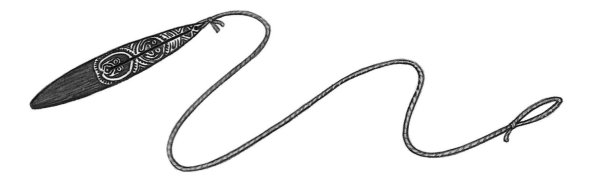

A bull roarer is also a wind instrument. The bull roarer makes a howling sound when it is whipped around and around in the air like a lasso. In this book, you will learn how to make a *garden-hose trumpet* and a *spoon roarer*.

Instruments with strings you can bow, pluck, or strum are called *string* instruments. The sitar is an unusual string instrument from India. It can have as many as twenty-seven strings, all vibrating at the same time, making an eerie sound. Using this book, you can make a *singing sitar*.

So be a one-person band, or ask your friends and family to join you. The main thing is to realize the joy of building and playing your own instruments. It is instantly rewarding.

Balloon Tom-Tom

Materials needed:

EMPTY JUICE CAN, OATMEAL BOX, POTATO-CHIP CAN, or other cylindrical container · CAN OPENER or SCISSORS · 2 LARGE BALLOONS · 2 HEAVY RUBBER BANDS · 2 PENCILS (with erasers)

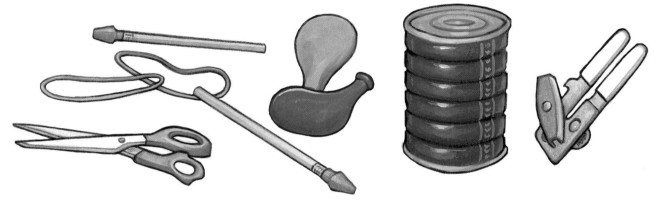

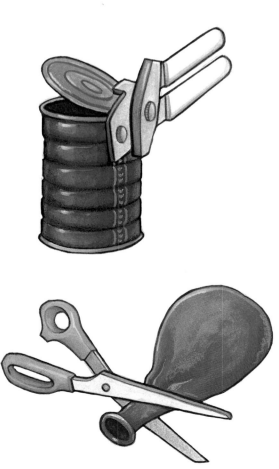

Putting it together:

1. If your container is open at only one end, use scissors or a can opener to open the other end of the container. This is the drum body.

2. Cut the open end off a large balloon.

3. Stretch the closed end of the balloon over one end of the drum body. The balloon is the drum skin.

4. Hold the balloon in place with a heavy rubber band and smooth out all the wrinkles to make the skin tight.

5. Repeat steps 2 to 4 on the other end of the drum body.

Now it's time to play your tom-tom. Pencils with erasers make great drumsticks, or use your fingers. Strike the skin around the rim or in the center to make different sounds. BOOM-BOOM-BOOM, RAP, RAP, RAP, BOOM-BOOM—and off you go!

Wrench Xylophone

Materials needed:

SET OF OPEN-ENDED WRENCHES · STRING · SCREWDRIVER

Putting it together:

1. Lay the wrenches out, arranging them from largest to smallest.

2. Tie the wrenches together with string at each end.

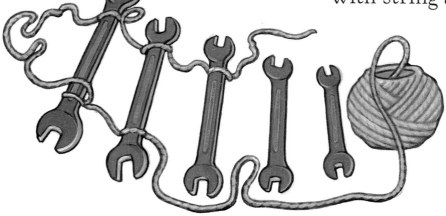

3. Tie a length of string to the ends of the largest wrench, and hang the xylophone up to play.

Now you can play your xylophone. A screwdriver handle makes a good striker. Hit the ends of each wrench, as well as the middle. The longer wrenches will make low sounds when played. Strike the shorter wrenches to make high sounds. Try adding a long loop to the bottom of the xylophone. Hold the loop firmly with your foot when you play. This gives the xylophone a very different sound. TONG, TONG, BONG, THUMMM . . .

Xylo-Drum

Materials needed:

TIN CAN, POTATO-CHIP CAN, FROZEN JUICE CONTAINER, or other cylindrical container · STYROFOAM CUP (with a base that will fit snugly into the open end of the container) · BALLOON · RUBBER BAND · 4–6 NAILS OF DIFFERENT SIZES (8, 10, 12 or 40, 50, 60 pennyweight; nails must be long enough to reach from one side of the cup to the other) · DUCT TAPE · CAN OPENER or SCISSORS · STICK

Putting it together:

1. Follow the instructions (steps 1 to 4) for the balloon tom-tom (pages 9–10) to make the drum body.

2. Lay out the nails, longest to shortest, and then push the nails in through the rim of the Styrofoam cup. Do not let the nails touch each other.

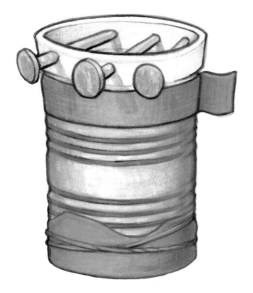

3. Fit the base of the cup into the open end of the drum body, then tape it in place.

4. Make a striker for the xylo-drum by taping a nail to a stick and wrapping tape around the other end of the stick.

With the nail end of the striker, hit the longer nails to make lower sounds, and the shorter nails for higher sounds. Bang on the balloon end with the taped end of the striker. Play one end at a time, or turn the xylo-drum on its side and play both ends at the same time. RING, TING, TING, BOOM, BOOM, BOOM . . . WOW—sounds great!

Garden-Hose Trumpet

Materials needed:

OLD PIECE OF GARDEN HOSE · SCISSORS · FUNNEL or PLASTIC SODA BOTTLE · DUCT TAPE

Putting it together:

1. Cut a length of old garden hose—a 3-foot length is a good piece with which to start. The longer and fatter the hose is, the harder it will be to blow through.

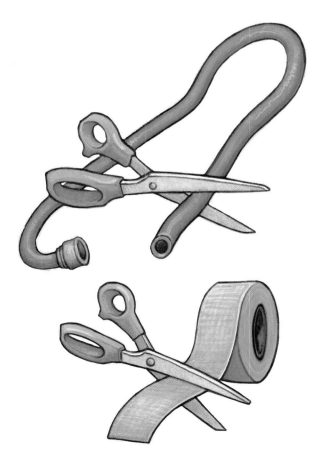

2. Cut a piece of duct tape 4 to 5 inches long.

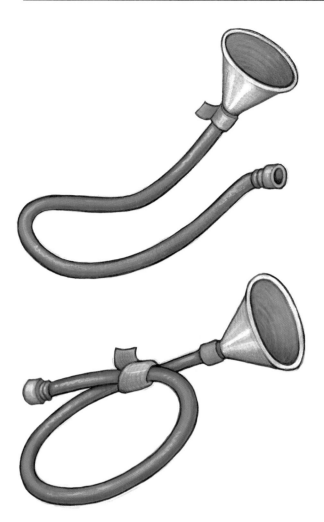

3. Insert the small end of a funnel into the cut end of the hose. Or cut the bottom off a soda bottle with scissors and insert the neck of the bottle into the cut end of the hose. Tape in place. The larger the funnel is, the louder the sound will be.

4. Coil the hose into a circle and hold in place with tape.

Squeeze your lips together tightly and blow into the hose. You can use the connector end of the hose as a mouthpiece, but you do not need to. Your lips will vibrate and wiggle fast together, and this may tickle. You can change the pitch by gently pinching the hose. TOOT, TOOT, TA-TOOT!

Spoon Roarer

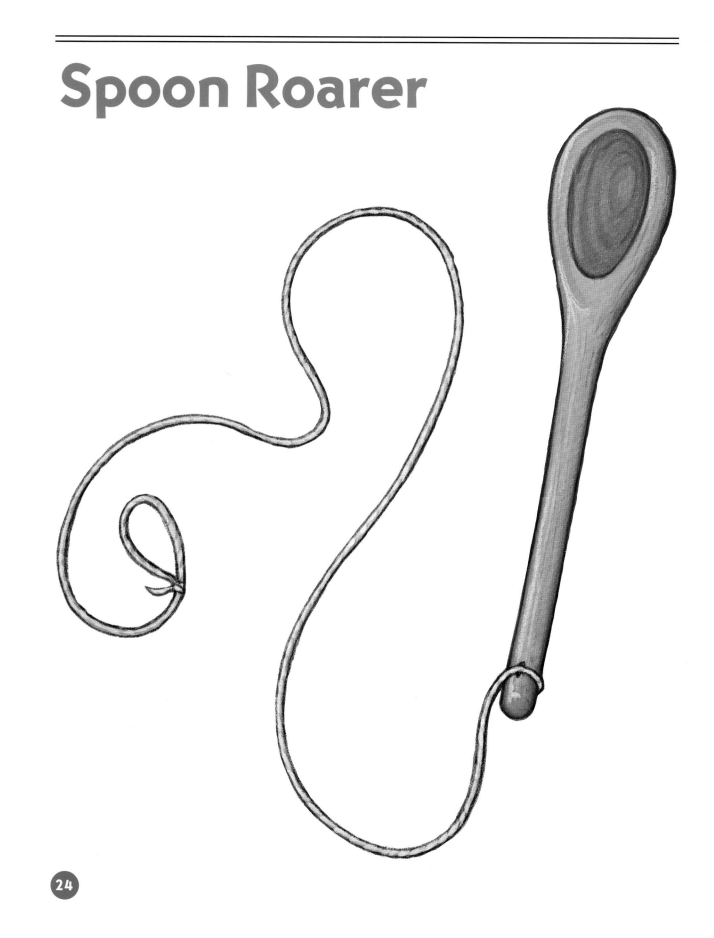

Materials needed:

WOODEN or PLASTIC KITCHEN SPOON (with a hole in the handle) · STRONG
STRING · SCISSORS

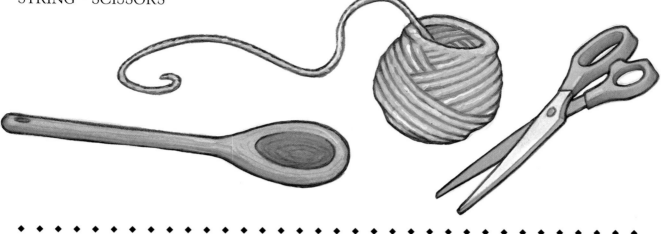

Putting it together:

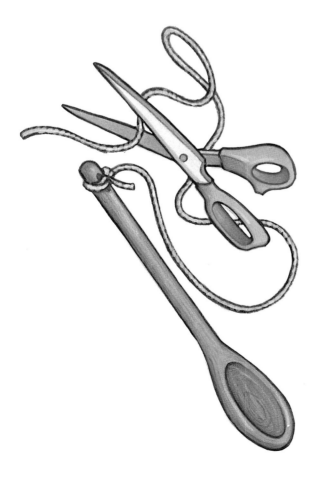

I. Thread one end of a long piece of string through the hole in the spoon handle and tie it very tightly, so there is no way the spoon can fly off the string. The length of string and spoon together should be a little shorter than you are tall.

2. Tie a loop at the other end of the string to hook your fingers through, or tie on another wooden spoon for a handle.

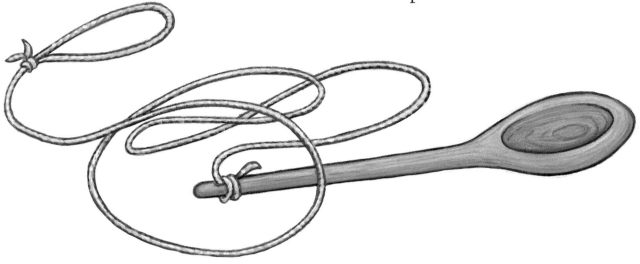

Before you play the spoon roarer, make sure you have lots of open space to swing it over your head without hitting anything or hurting anybody. Hold the loop end of the string tightly and twirl the spoon a little bit, and then let out the string and spin the spoon over your head like a lasso. Whirr away, and surprise people with your spoon roarer's unusual sounds. WHIRR, WHIRR, WHIRR, SWISH, WHIRR . . .

Singing Sitar

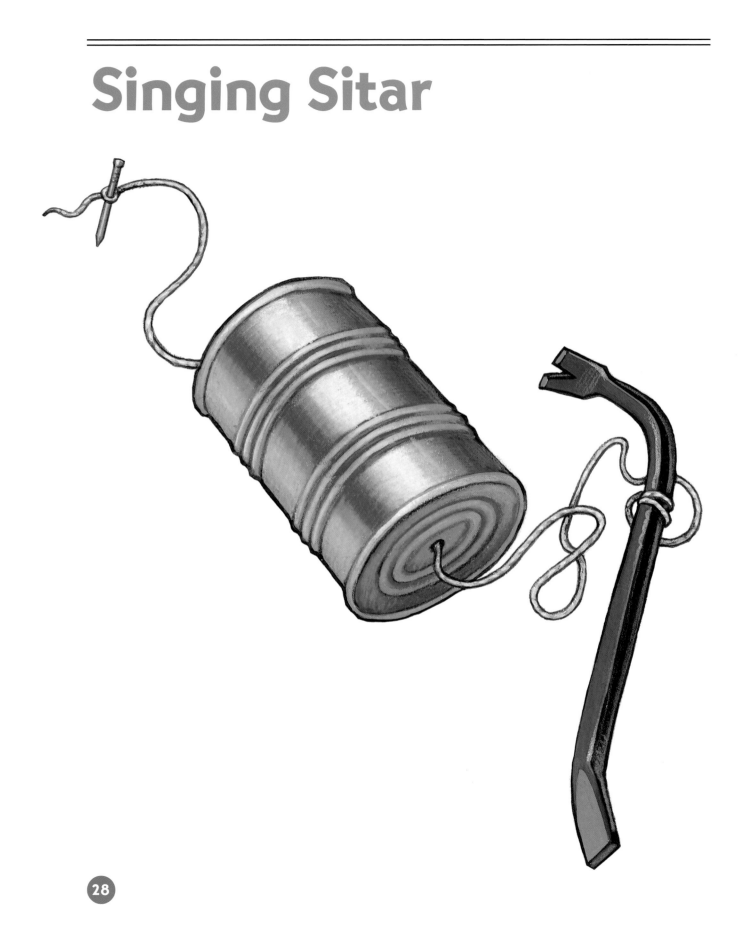

Materials needed:

EMPTY CAN · NAIL · HAMMER · COTTON, NYLON, or METAL STRING · CROW-BAR, METAL PIPE, HAMMER, or other heavy weight · COAT HANGER, STICK, or PENCIL · SCISSORS

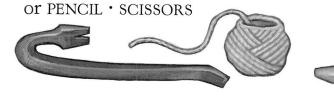

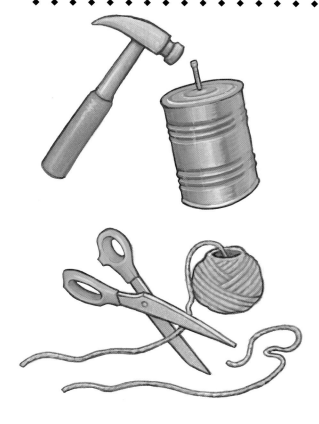

Putting it together:

1. Ask an adult to help you punch a hole through the center of the bottom of the can and two others, one on either side near the top rim of the can, using a nail and a hammer.

2. Cut two lengths of string, each about 3 feet long.

3. Thread one string through the hole in the bottom of the can. Tie a nail to the end of the string inside the can so it will not come out through the hole.

4. Tie a heavy weight such as a crowbar, a metal pipe, or a hammer to the free end of the string. Or try a bucket of water!

5. Thread the other length of string through the holes at the top of the can and tie the ends together, to make a handle.

One way to play the sitar is to hold the handle with one hand and drape the weighted string loosely over the edge of a worktable. Or, for a different sound, hang the sitar over the branch of a tree, or in a doorway, so that the weighted string hangs down from the can. Let the weight hang freely to pull the string tight.

Pluck the string with your fingers or tap it with a pencil, stick, coat hanger, or a screwdriver handle. Listen to the string and the can humming their own tunes. Pull the string as you pluck. It will sing in many voices.

TWANG away . . . TWANG, TWWAANNGG . . .

Now that you have made all these instruments, you can play them by yourself, or have your own band! These are only a few suggestions out of many possibilities. Invent your own instruments.

You will be amazed by what you discover!

784.192   Oates, Eddie
O   Herschel.

        Making music.

                        XG5220510
$14.89

DATE			

Clear Stream Avenue School Library
U.F.S. Dist. #30
Valley Stream, N.Y. 11580

BAKER & TAYLOR